Teacher

Lucy M. George

Ando Twin

Ms. Betts is a teacher. She bicycles to school early in the morning and waves hello to Andy, the crossing guard.

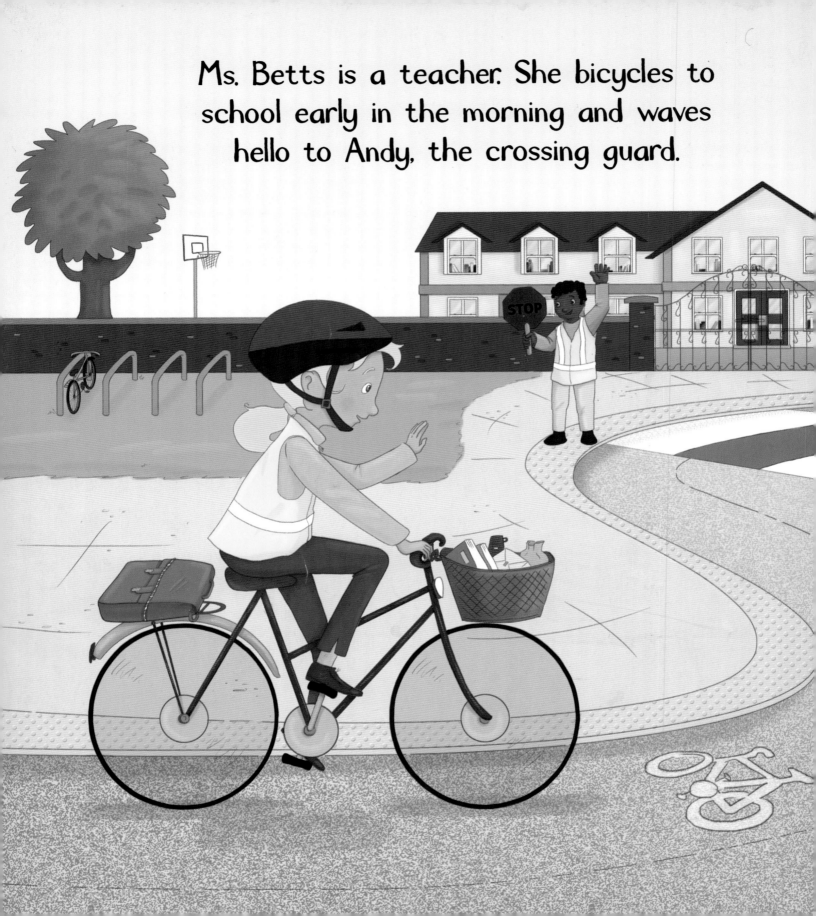

Before the children arrive, Ms. Betts gets everything ready for the day.

Mr. Fletcher, the teacher's assistant, asks what he can do to help.

It's time for school to start. The bell rings and the children come in and sit down.

Monday 5th

"Good morning, Ms. Betts!" they say together.

Ms. Betts has some exciting news. A very special guest is coming to visit the class this afternoon.

But first, Mr. Fletcher takes the children to the school assembly.

Today the Principal tells them to always try their best and not give up.

In the morning,
Ms. Betts
teaches math.

After recess,
the children go
to the library.

Then they go back to class
to paint pictures.

Finally, it's lunchtime!

Ms. Betts encourages Sophie to try some peas
and helps Toby find his lunch box.

"I'd better go meet our special guest now!"
says Ms. Betts with a smile.

The special guest is Kelly Jones,
a local athlete and 100-meter dash gold medalist!

The children are very excited! They hurry into
their gym clothes and go out to the field.

Kelly shows them how to do jumping jacks . . .

. . . and push ups to warm up.

Then they have a race.

"Try your best and don't give up!" Kelly shouts.

Afterward, they sit on the grass and ask Kelly questions.

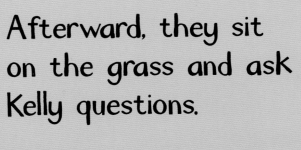

She tells them what it's like to be an athlete . . .

. . . how she won her gold medal . . .

. . . and what kinds of food she eats to stay healthy.

"Do you want to try on my medal?" she asks.

There's time for one more race—
between the grown-ups!

The Principal comes
out to watch.

Kelly Jones wins the race!

"Hooray!" everyone cheers.

Back in the classroom, Ms. Betts
reads the children a story . . .

. . . and then it is time to go home.

The children wave
good-bye to Ms. Betts
and Mr. Fletcher.

"See you tomorrow, everyone!"
Ms. Betts says.

Mr. Fletcher helps Ms. Betts clean up and they talk about their plans for tomorrow. It's going to be another busy day!

On her way home, Ms. Betts has to ride up a big hill. Some days she has to stop because it's very steep.

But she remembers Kelly Jones saying,

"Try your best and don't give up!"

And guess what?

Today, she makes it all the way to the top of the hill!

What else does Ms. Betts do?

Writes
reports.

Meets with
parents.

Plans
lessons.

Corrects
homework.

Puts the children's
work on display.

What does Ms. Betts need?

1 x 2 = 2
2 x 2 = 4
3 x 2 = 6
4 x 2 = 8
5 x 2 = 10

Whiteboard

Marker pens

Workbooks

Big bag

Scissors

Laptop

Pens and pencils

Glue

Staple gun

Other busy people

Here are some of the other busy people teachers work with.

Teachers' assistants help the children with their work during lessons. They also help the teacher to prepare materials and clean up.

Principals are in charge of running the school. They meet with parents and other teachers to make sure all the children are happy and learning.

Lunchtime monitors help the school chefs serve meals for the children and staff. They also help to look after the children in the cafeteria and on the playground.

Crossing guards help children to cross the road safely on their way to school and on their way back home.

Next steps

- Discuss the similarities and differences between the children's own school day and the school day in the story. What activity is their favorite at school?

- Explain some of the things you do to prepare for class each day. How do the children prepare for class?

- Give the children an opportunity to ask you questions about what it is like to be a teacher. Would any of the children like to be teachers one day?

- Invite the Principal or another school employee to visit your class and share what happens during their day.

- In the story, both the Principal and Kelly Jone tell the children to try their hardest and not give up. Ask the children if they have ever tried really hard at something.

- The children and adults in the story race! Plan a class race or a teacher race.

Publisher: Zeta Jones
Associate Publisher: Maxime Boucknooghe
Editorial Director: Victoria Garrard
Art Director: Laura Roberts-Jensen
Editor: Sophie Hallam
Designer: Anna Lubecka

JJ
GEORGE
LUCY

First published in the United States by
QEB Publishing, Inc.
6 Orchard
Lake Forest, CA 92630

www.qed-publishing.co.uk

A CIP record for this book is available from the Library of Congress.

ISBN 978 1 60992 832 2

Printed in China

**For Granny Wilson
—AndoTwin**

**For Milo Theodore Bet
—Lucy M.George**